S0-BIN-575

150 Best Minimalist House Ideas

150 Best Minimalist House Ideas

HARPER
DESIGN
An Imprint of HarperCollinsPublishers

150 BEST MINIMALIST HOUSE IDEAS
Copyright © 2013 by HARPER DESIGN and LOFT Publications

First published in 2013 by:
Harper Design
An Imprint of HarperCollins*Publishers*
10 East 53rd Street
New York, NY 10022
Tel.: (212) 207-7000
Fax: (212) 207-7654
harperdesign@harpercollins.com
www.harpercollins.com

Distributed throughout the world by:
HarperCollins*Publishers*
10 East 53rdStreet
New York, NY 10022
Fax: (212) 207-7654

Editorial coordinator: Claudia Martínez Alonso
Assistant to editorial coordination: Ana Marques
Art director: Mireia Casanovas Soley
Editor: Àlex Sánchez Vidiella
Text: Francesc Zamora Mola
Layout: Cristina Simó Perales
Cover layout: María Eugenia Castell Carballo

ISBN: 978-0-06-231547-2

Library of Congress Control Number: 2013954400

Printed in China
First printing, 2013

CONTENTS

Introduction

Minimalism implies the reduction of all elements to a minimum and essential level, achieving spaces that are clutter free and free of excessive decoration. If you are looking to simplify your home, and give it a sophisticated look, a minimalist style might be what you are looking for. This book features a rich selection of architecture and interior design projects, and 150 ideas we hope will spur your imagination to design your home in a minimalist style.

A minimalist home strives for order and harmony in the relationship between spaces and the objects they contain. Space flows continuously around walls. Living, dining, and kitchen spaces leak into each other. Often walls are used not to partition a space into rooms, but rather to create segments of space within the larger volume. Another option is to compartmentalize a space with movable panels and screens.

In minimalist homes, the boundaries between interior and exterior spaces are blurred. The reflective and transparent properties of metal and glass are used to give the impression of a dematerialization of the building. This is how architecture and landscape become a single item.

From an aesthetic view, free-flowing spaces suggest the disposition of the positive and negative, and the transformation of architectural forms into synthetic shapes enhances the visual power of light and color. The easiest way to describe minimalist spaces is by showing examples. Rejecting unnecessary detailing and decoration in favor of open space, Belgian architect Karla Menten in her Hidden apartment remodel, emptied out its interior. Then, inspired by the suprematist compositions of Kazimir Malevich, she inserted three volumes, which contain the essential home equipment and introduce a touch of color. As a result, the apartment is spare—or, as she puts it, has "an elementally ethereal aesthetic."

Artist Donald Judd's long arrangements of repeated geometric objects are another well-known illustration of minimalist composition. Judd's simple but powerful arrangements divide space in a clean, architectural manner. Like columns, the objects structure and define the area surrounding them. Visually, their full effect depends on the presence of light or, more specifically, the play of light and shadow.

As the most immaterial of architectural elements, light enlivens and transforms architecture and interior spaces. The ephemeral, time-sensitive qualities that light produces on surfaces was clearly understood by American minimalist artist Dan Flavin, who said that, "A piece of wall can be visually disintegrated from the whole into a separate triangle by plunging a diagonal of light from edge to edge on the wall."

Although one inevitably thinks of white when discussing minimalist architecture and inter ior design, the interplay of form and light is completed by color. The use of a highly limited color palette responds to the need to reduce everything to a bare minimum for its powerful effect, especially when combined with form and light, reiterating that "less is more."

House on a Castle Mountainside

Architect: Fran Silvestre,
Mª José Sáez/
Fran Silvestre Arquitectos

Location: Ayora, Spain

Photography: Fernando Alda

The house is located at the base of a cliff with an ancient castle atop. Its architects avoided mimetic designs and its all-white appearance makes it stand out from its rugged surroundings, but it does not fight the neighboring houses.

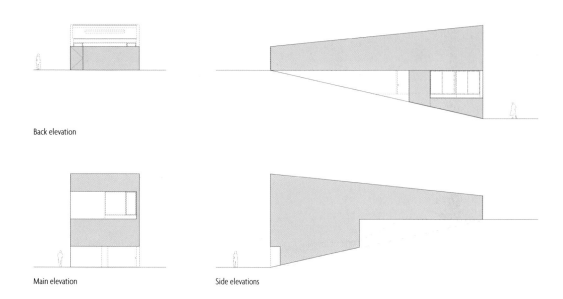

Back elevation

Main elevation   Side elevations

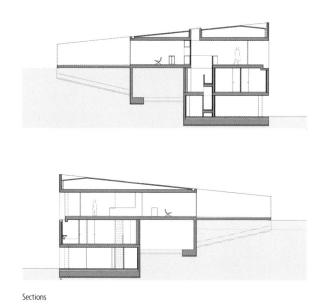

Sections

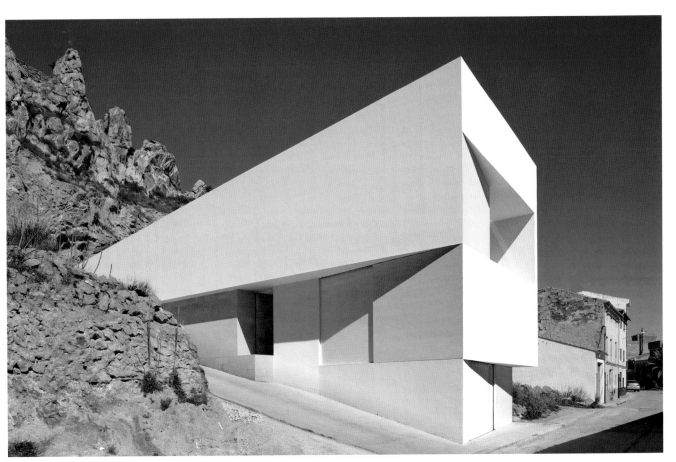

From outside the house looks like a wedge sunk into the rocky hillside. Inside, the layout is stratified and organized around a vertical communication nucleus that also brings light in.

001

Dramatic visual effects can be achieved by the incidence of light on forms—changing not only the atmosphere, but also the perception of the geometry.

002

In minimalist architecture, components often serve both visual and functional purposes. For instance, a kitchen block can provide a nice visual break-up to a room and also divide spaces with different purposes.

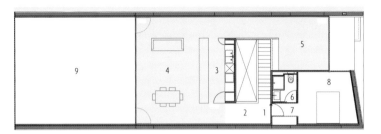

Third floor plan

1. Stair
2. Vestibule
3. Kitchen
4. Living-dining room
5. Study
6. Bathroom 2
7. Vestibule
8. Bedroom 3
9. Terrace

Second floor plan

1. Stair
2. Entry hall
3. Vestibule
4. Bathroom 1
5. Bedroom 1
6. Bedroom 2

First floor plan

1. Garage
2. Laundry room
3. Vestibule
4. Cellar

003

A small bathroom can look bigger when accessed through a narrow corridor. Play with differing light intensities to emphasize this effect.

Godiva House

This home was designed to meet the needs of a person with reduced mobility and to be environmentally sustainable. It has two interconnected rectangular volumes oriented by the triangular nature of the plot. The spatial identity of the house lies in the dialog between its interior and exterior.

Architect: EMPTY SPACE Architecture
Location: Cascais, Portugal
Photography: João Morgado

A glass volume provides entry to the house, is the connector between the two larger structures, and dictates the home's spatial organization.

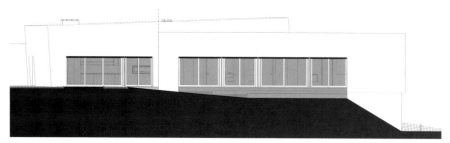

Main elevation

Back elevation

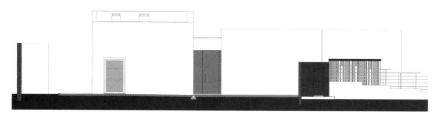

Left side elevation

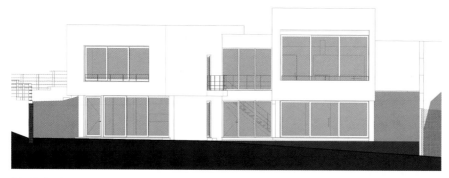

Right side elevation

004

Low-E glass provides protection against harmful sun rays, and is energy efficient because it achieves a balance between capturing and reflecting solar heat.

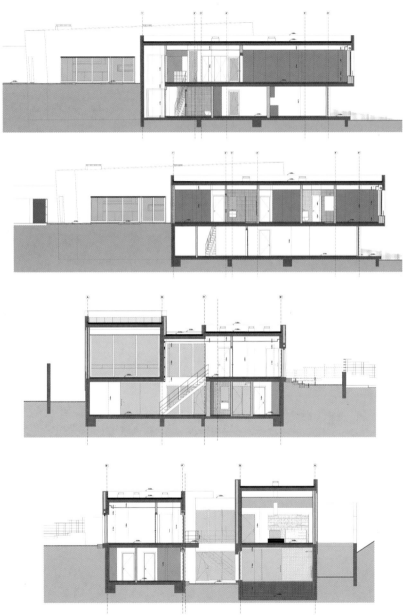

Sections

005

A simple geometry, a limited set of materials, and a reduced color palette can still produce dynamic architecture with a high level of detailing.

006

A staircase is a critical architectural element, and its design should harmonize with the general design theme. It can either be fully integrated in the main structure or can stand as an inserted object.

007

Large pieces of art should accent the space they reside in, not fight against it. Artwork that takes up the full height of a wall will make a ceiling seem lower.

008

Make your fireplace the focus of your living area. If given a central position, it can be enjoyed from different sides, while at the same time separating spaces with unique functions.

009

A kitchen island is a work surface, but can also be a place to display your favorite objects.

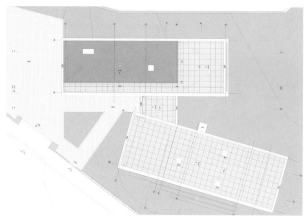

Roof plan

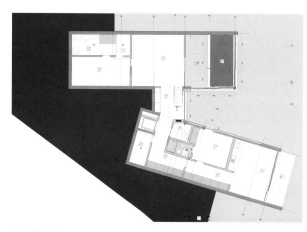

Lower floor plan

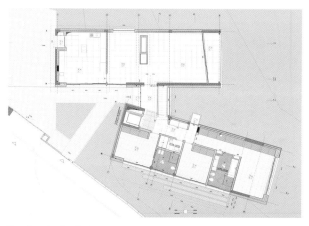

Upper floor plan. Entry level

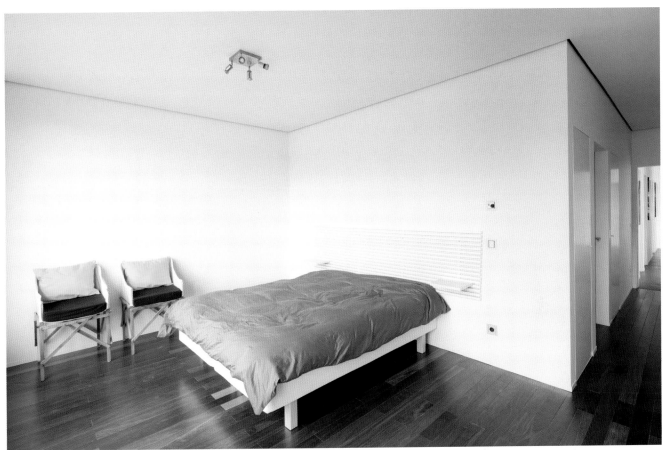

Can Manuel d'en Corda

An old stone house near a forest of pine trees and junipers was the base of this remodel project. The vernacular architecture of the original structure, with its dry-set stone walls and pitched roof, had a design typical of Formentera. The remodeled home satisfies the current building regulations while preserving the integrity of the original structure. As well, the impact of the redesign on the environment was kept to a minimum.

Architect: Marià Castelló + Daniel Redolat
Location: Formentera, Spain
Photography: Estudi Es Pujol de s'Era

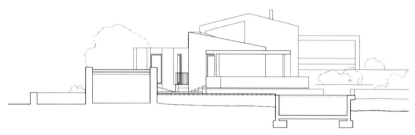

Northeast elevation

Cross section

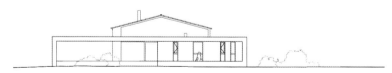

Southwest elevation

The new architecture was purposefully fragmented and staggered. It is attached to the original structure's northeast and southwest sides. The southeast and northwest walls were left intact.

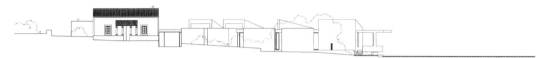

Southeast elevation

Northwest elevation

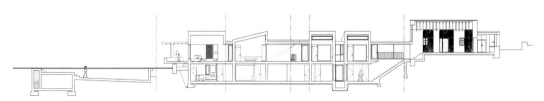

Longitudinal section

010

Porches and patios can be airy interstitial spaces, linking different parts of a fragmented house. They articulate a house's form by joining the interior and exterior.

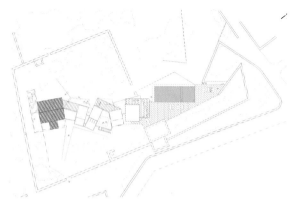

Roof plan

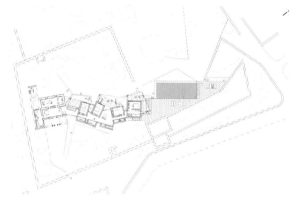

Ground floor plan

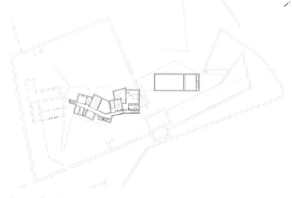

Basement floor plan

Whitewash is a painting technique used to whiten a surface. It is often applied to exterior walls and the roofs of houses in rural areas.

011

Rustic and modern designs are compatible. Stone walls give an attractive artisanal look and make for a great backdrop behind a collection of contemporary furniture and accessories.

012

Create a simple yet
sophisticated bedroom with
minimal materials and finishes:
crisp white surfaces, exposed
concrete, and limestone floors.
Add warmth with wood window
and door frames.

013

The geometry of a trough-like washbasin adds to a minimalist bathroom design. It can be made from glass, marble, ceramic, or polished concrete.

Amalia House

Architect: Marià Castelló
Location: Formentera, Spain
Photography: Estudi
Es Pujol de s'Era

Located on the south coast of the island of Formentera, this house is the result of a remodel that combined contemporary design and the vernacular style of the island. The house is composed of a series of cubes with thick walls to keep the searing heat out, and flat roofs that were once used for water collection. The architecture, simple and refined, is open to the natural environment and views of the sea.

Existing conditions. North elevation

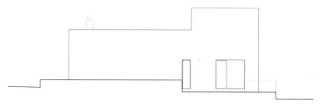

Remodel. North elevation

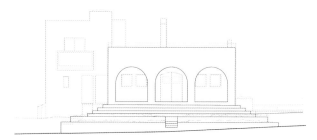

Existing conditions. South elevation

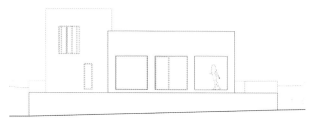

Remodel. South elevation

014

In hot climates, a sheltered porch or veranda is a must-have architectural feature. This covered space shades a house and catches natural ventilation.

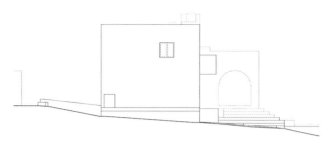

Existing conditions. West elevation

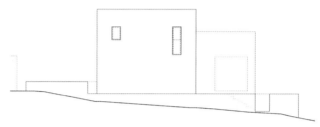

Remodel. West elevation

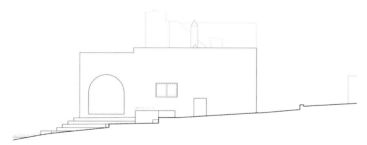

Existing conditions. East elevation

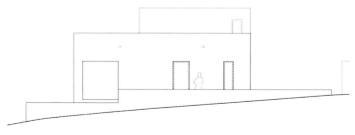

Remodel. East elevation

015

A porch that "works" provides bioclimatic and aesthetic benefits.

016

Continuous flooring connecting indoor and outdoor spaces can cause problems with rainwater filtering. Weather-stripping doors and a roof over the exterior space will solve this.

Limestone floors, plaster finish on the walls and ceiling, white-lacquered medium-density fiberboard (MDF) furniture, and synthetic white quartz panels were used on this house to homogenize the existing structure with the new construction.

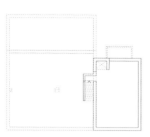

Existing conditions. Roof plan

Remodel. Roof plan

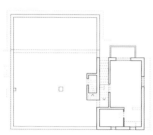

Existing conditions. Upper floor plan

Remodel. Upper floor plan

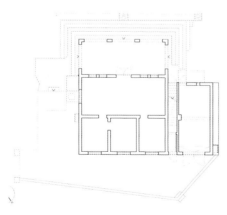

Existing conditions. Lower floor plan

Remodel. Lower floor plan

017

Sliding panels were used to partition the space, dividing it into areas with unique functions.

018

If privacy is not an issue,
a washbasin can be placed
outside of the bathroom.

8x8 House

This project consisted of the extension of an existing house located on the western side of the Spanish island Formentera. The rustic landscape guided the design. A new annex is composed of two sections. There is a spacious, public living room and a kitchen separated by sliding panels. A more private section includes an office, a bedroom, and a bathroom.

Architect: Marià Castelló
Location: Formentera, Spain
Photography: Lourdes Grivé,
EPDSE

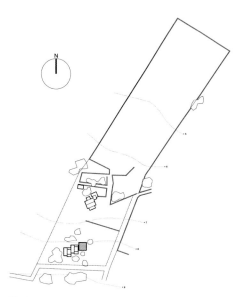

Site plan

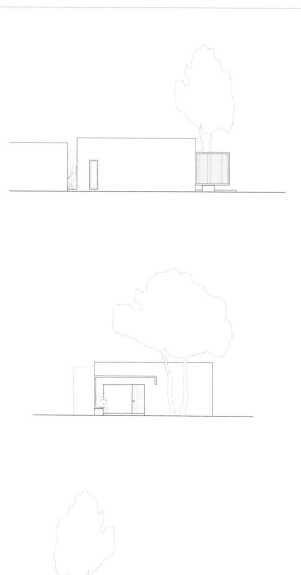

Elevations

The new construction is accessible through a deck, which is protected from the strong sunlight by an L-shaped canopy. The canopy is made of square steel tubing painted white to match the house.

019

Sliding panels can be custom
sized and made of nearly any
rigid material.

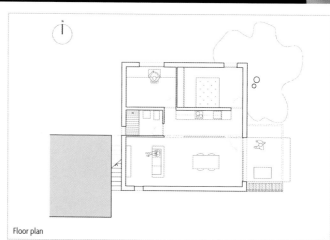

Floor plan

020

Add texture if a bathroom seems too cold or sterile. Use wood to create a more natural and inviting feeling, but don't overdo it—doing so would interfere with a clean look.

Dwelling at Maytree

This two-story house is a bold sculptural form that replaced a derelict 1940s single-story cottage. Sitting at the foot of a steep escarpment, it is accessed via a long processional path. The hallway in the main entry level of the house was conceived of as an "internal street." Its dimensions widen at the more public realms of the plan, and diminish in the private areas.

Architect: ODOS architects
Location: Wicklow, Ireland
Photography: Ros Kavanagh and ODOS architects

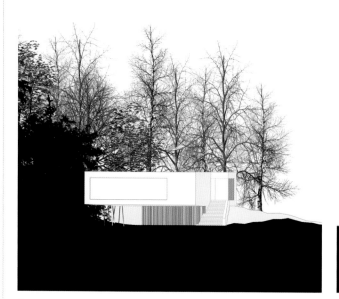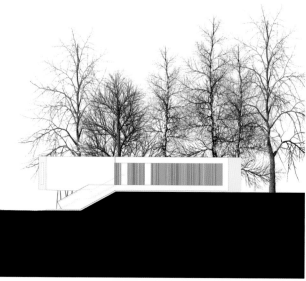

Elevations

Red columns below the cantilevered
volume mark a pedestrian path wedged
between the house and the base of the
escarpment. The path leads to the rear
garden and living room deck.

021

A tapering staircase gives glamour to the entryway. The varying tread size creates a false perspective that magnifies the stair's length.

022

Bring a little zing to a monochromatic room with colorful furnishings. Here, green-yellow armchairs harmonize with the landscape, blurring the boundary between interior and exterior.

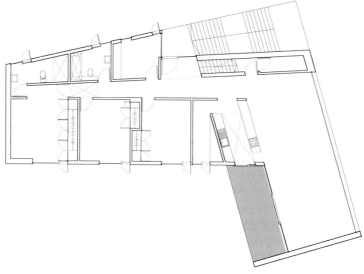

Ground floor plan

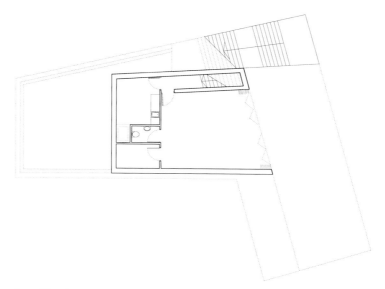

Basement floor plan

023

Transform a hallway into an art gallery. Ascertain the balance between natural and artificial lighting to optimize the display of the art.

Suntro House

Suntro House has an asymmetrical and undulating skin enveloping an open-plan layout. It is a building where the exterior generates the interior, rather than the, more common, other way around. A generous amount of glass filters natural light during the day and emits a bright glow at night, producing a stark contrast of light and dark shadows.

Architect: Jorge Hernández de la Garza

Location: Oaxtepec, Mexico

Photography: Paul Czitrom

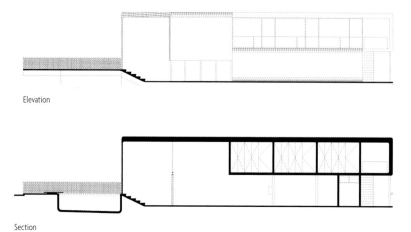

Elevation

Section

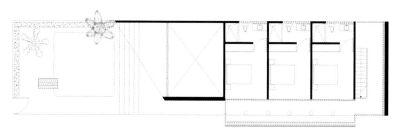

Upper floor plan

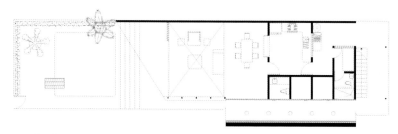

Lower floor plan

024

Light and shadow emphasizes form and texture. As the Danish architect Steen Eiler Rasmussen said, "Light is of decisive importance in experiencing architecture."

The design of the house ensures an indoor-outdoor connection. Its orientation encourages cooling air to flow across the space, and the large glassed-in surfaces allow visual interaction with its natural surroundings.

025

Do not saturate a room with colors and patterns if you want to achieve a soothing minimalist atmosphere. Instead let the materials sing for themselves.

Reykjavik House

Architect: Jakub Majewski,
Łukasz Pastuszka/
Moomoo Architects

Location: Reykjavik, Iceland

Photography: Moomoo
Architects

This smart white house blends with Reykjavik's snowy landscape. Making the most of views and its isolated location, the house has two fully glazed walls and a deck. Two large skylights over the living area add an architectural element and brighten the room even further.

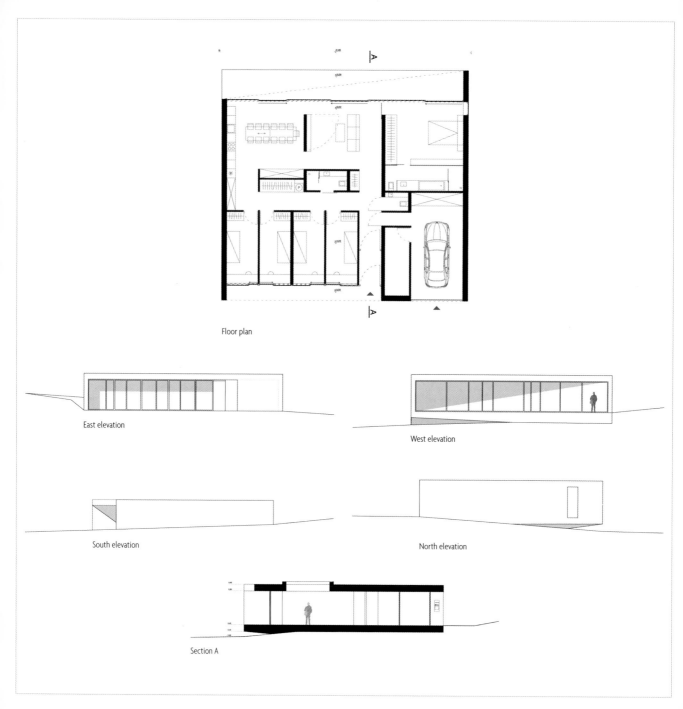

Floor plan

East elevation

West elevation

South elevation

North elevation

Section A

026

Take advantage of sliding glass doors, which allow for almost uninterrupted panoramic views. With a minimal amount of visible support, they can handle high wind loads.

027

Floor-to-ceiling sliding windows allow the house to be opened up during the warm months of the year, blurring the boundaries between interior and exterior.

The garage, living area, master bedroom, and children's bedrooms have independent access to the exterior. This is achieved by concentrating utility spaces at the center of the house, instead of around it.

028

The size of a skylight determines the lighting level and the temperature of the room below. In choosing one, consider which type of skylight would best contribute to your home's energy efficiency.

This project consists of two structures carefully inserted within the construction limits, respecting the genius loci of the site. The unique geometries of these structures respond to the different functions that each of them accommodates. Nonetheless they are all part of a whole. The physical connections between them are established by means of interstitial spaces.

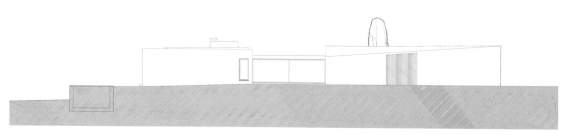

East elevation

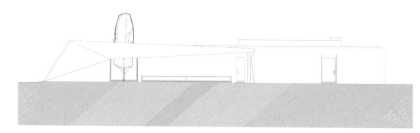

North elevation

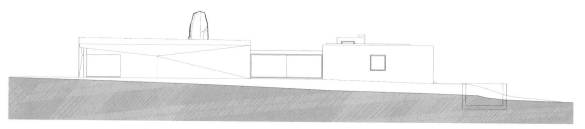

West elevation

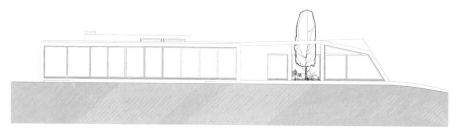

South elevation

029

Architecture and landscape complement each other. With fewer elements to distract, the relationship between the building and the site where it stands is stronger.

030

Before choosing your windows, learn about energy efficient architectural tools like U-values, Low-E glass, and weather stripping, especially if you are planning on using large expanses of glass.

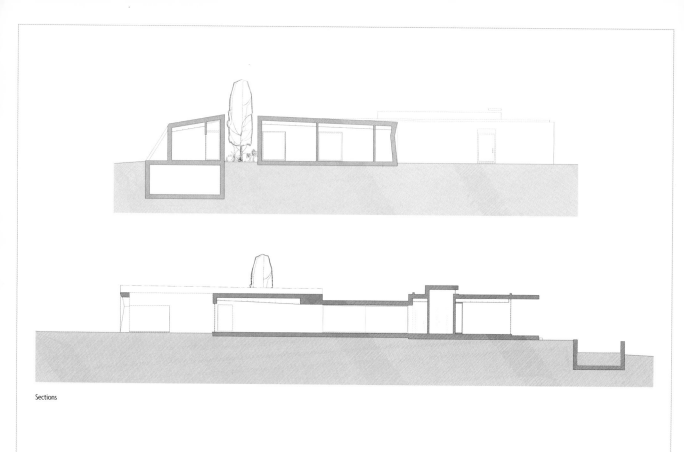

Sections

031

A hardscape of marble chips
can complement a simple
geometric building. Plants
and well-defined green areas
are also perfectly suitable
additions.

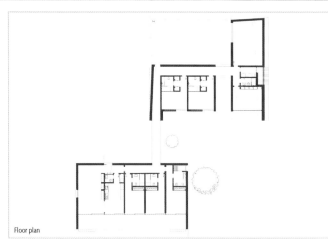

Floor plan

032

Unobstructed sight lines give an interior space a sense of continuity and produce a very pleasant Zen-like impression.

033

The appeal of a strikingly
geometric exterior can be
extended to the design of
interior spaces by means of
built-in furniture, which adapts
to the shapes of the building.

The design of the vanity echoes the planar geometry of the bathroom and mimics the color palette based on white, gray, and beige tones.

Smooth Building

Architect: Jorge Hernández
de la Garza
Location: Nuevo León, Mexico
Photography: Paul Czitrom

The design of this house was dictated by a request from the client that the structure accommodate both work and living uses. The architect faced a challenge in organizing the mix-use program: to provide privacy, while at the same time opening the building to the views of the majestic Sierra Madre mountain range. The design effort resulted in a homogeneous and transparent construction with sculptural qualities.

The office, which occupies the first two floors of the building, features glass partitions and rays of recessed lighting.

Second floor plan

Third floor plan

Main floor plan

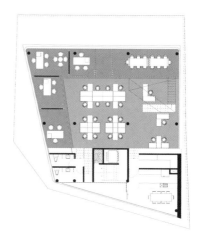

First floor plan

034

Emphasize singular
architectural pieces at
night through transparent
elements and lighting.

The two uppermost floors are reserved for domestic uses. The living room is a double-height space that opens onto a terrace with views of the mountain range on the horizon.

035

Durable and resistant, high-gloss laminate is a good choice for a sleek kitchen. Cabinet push-latches can replace handles to add to a modern design.

Atrium House

Two strategies were used to give this house a sense of spaciousness. One was to leave the center of the site unbuilt in order to create a space with strong interior-exterior connections. This was achieved by making the walls facing this inner courtyard all glass. The second strategy was to bring light into the basement. This was done by taking advantage of the terrain's slope.

Architect: Fran Silvestre,
Mª José Sáez/
Fran Silvestre Arquitectos

Location: Godella, Spain

Photography: Fernando Alda

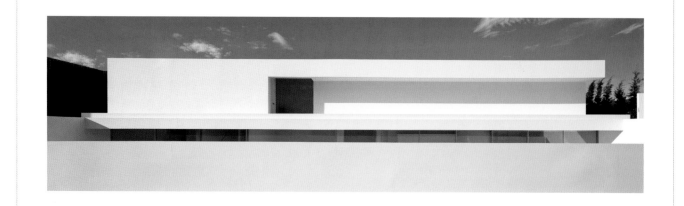

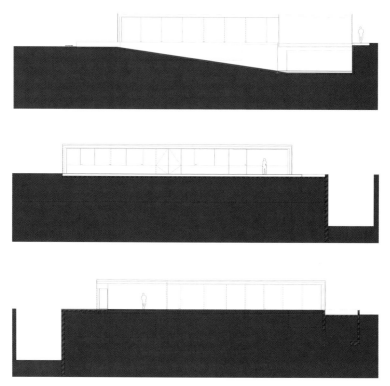

Elevations

036

By using a monochromatic
color scheme, emphasis is put
on form, and light and shadow
contrasts are accentuated.

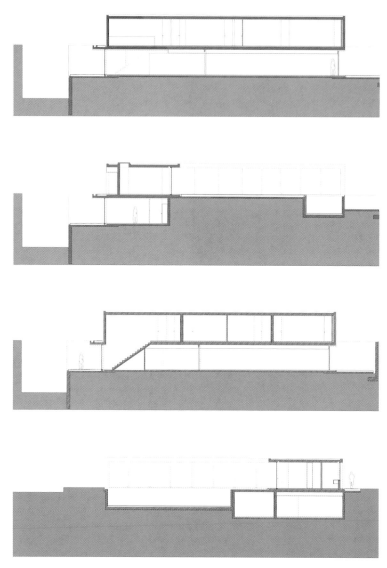

Sections

037

Transparent and opaque surfaces create a dynamic design guided by forms. Long horizontal planes emphasize perspective.

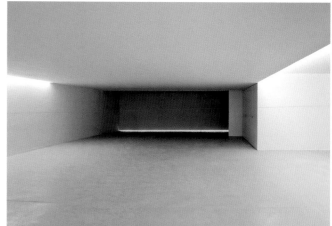

038

In monochromatic spaces, light can produce serenity, comfort, and intrigue.

039

Richly colored and textured furnishings are a great accent in all-white spaces. Sparse wood pieces in their natural finishes complement minimalist décor nicely.

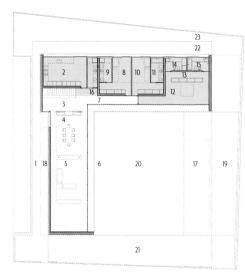

1. Main access
2. Kitchen
3. Stairs
4. Dining room
5. Living room
6. Covered terrace
7. Corridor
8. Bedroom / Dressing room 1
9. Bathroom
10. Bedroom / Dressing room 2
11. Bathroom
12. Master bedroom
13. Master dressing room
14. Main bathroom 3
15. Main bathroom 4
16. Toilet
17. Swimming pool
18. Covered access
19. Car access
20. Atrium
21. Front garden
22. Rear terrace
23. Rear garden

Upper floor plan

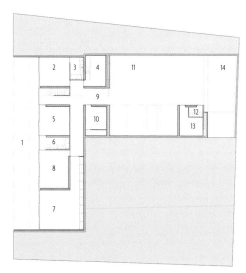

1. Courtyard
2. Laundry room
3. Bathroom
4. Utility room
5. Bedroom
6. Bathroom
7. Gymnasium
8. Study-library
9. Corridor
10. Wine cellar
11. Garage
12. Toilet
13. Workshop
14. Garage ramp

Lower floor plan

The intersection of the house's two wings is where the staircase, kitchen, and laundry room are, along with the core of the house's utility spaces.

040

Small reveals between the
floor, walls, and ceilings
emphasize planar surfaces
over mass. This effect is most
visible under artificial lighting.

Darie House

From the outside, it isn't clear that this structure of great modularity is a house. The planar design of the front façade creates an asymmetrical composition that highlights the sides of the building, revealing its volume. The façade regularly changes thanks to a system of shutters that pivot. At certain angles, it offers views that cross the interior of the building—all the way to its back end.

Architect: Pitsou Kedem
Architecture
Location: Kfar Shmaryahu, Israel
Photography: Amit Geron

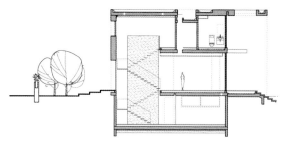

Section

Upper floor plan

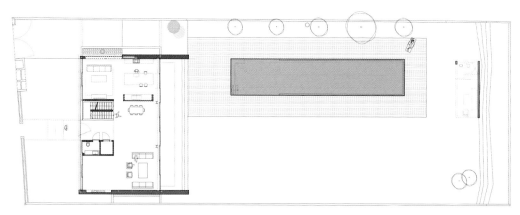

Lower floor plan

When the shutters are fully open and the interior is exposed, the exquisitely simple but intricate detailing of the construction is revealed.

041

Blinds, shutters, and other changeable architectural elements that define the perimeter of a space can create a dynamic relationship between the interior and the exterior.

Spaces characterized by a
restrained use of materials
often rely on light to create
a sense of movement and
provide character.

043

Precast concrete is a versatile material with a plasticity that adds visual interest and depth to walls. It has the capacity to utilize various finishes and colors, and be produced in any shape.

House in Cala Bassa

Architect: DUE
Architecture + Design
Location: Cala Bassa, Spain
Photography: DUE
Architecture + Design

This house is a white cuboid with floor-to-ceiling glass doors, and deep-set windows. These elements emphasize the massiveness of the structure and were carefully placed to allow a pleasant breeze throughout the house.

044

Even a minimalist home can have splashes of color and contrast. Create these effects with carefully selected furnishings and accessories.

Main elevation

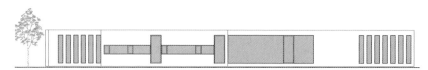

Back elevation

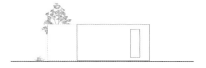

Left side elevation

Right side elevation

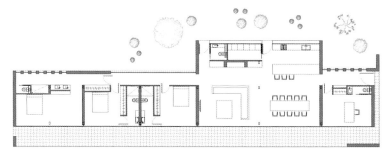

Floor plan

045

Open shelves in the kitchen offer the opportunity to introduce color and texture in the form of glass jars filled with herbs and spices.

046

Pivot doors are an alternative
to hinged doors, and are
generally used without a
door frame. The pivot system
accommodates large doors,
which can be operated with
little effort.

047

A small, awkward corner can be turned into a powder room or vanity.

Kapoor House

This house opens up to incredible panoramic views. Its simple design with a minimal palette of materials such as concrete, stucco, wood, stone, and stainless steel, accommodates a complex program while avoiding ostentation. From the frameless windows to the trimless, recessed LED lights, the house is characterized by a precise level of detail.

Architect: Swatt | Miers Architects
Location: Berkeley, CA, USA
Photography: Tim Griffith

048

Use seemless glass panel
guardrails to maximize views.

049

Wood can be a good finish for a ceiling and is an alternative to a painted finish. Like hardwood floors, a wood ceiling provides a sense of warmth and comfort.

050

Clerestories or high windows visually separate the walls from the ceiling, providing an effect of lightness. Because they are high up in the wall, privacy is maintained.

051

Sliding panels can dramatically transform a space. They can be used to close off large openings or separate spaces with different functions.

Secret House

Aware of the potential of a site overlooking the skyline of Kuwait, the owners of this home, a young couple with children, wanted a house oriented inward at street level and gradually opening out to produce broad views of the skyline on the upper levels. As a result, the house has various degrees of privacy.

Architect: AGI Architects
Location: Shuwaikh, Kuwait
Photography: Nelson Garrido

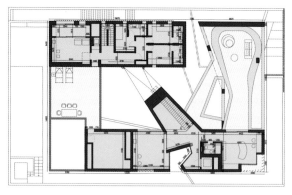

Second floor plan

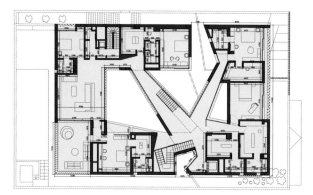

First floor plan

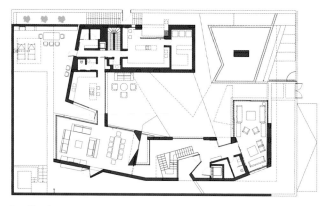

Ground floor plan

The distances between houses in harsh, desert-like climates are shorter than most. This is done to create narrow shaded spaces, which work as passive temperature regulators.

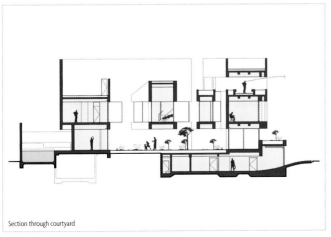

Section through courtyard

052

Plan your outdoor seating arrangements the way you would a living room. A good set-up will make it easy to use the space in the event of parties or family gatherings— even impromptu ones.

053

Roller shades are an alternative to curtains. They use a minimal amount of fabric, and are available in varying levels of opacity.

Eriso House

Architect: Agraz Arquitectos
Location: Fraccionamiento
Los Jales, Mexico
Photography: Mito Covarrubias

Surrounded by gardens on three sides, this house stands on an elevated site above the street and turns its fourth wall to an adjacent property. It utilizes two floors above an underground garage, and embraces a harmonious array of volumes. During its design, the outdoor and indoor areas received an equal amount of attention, so the designers could make sure that architecture and landscape complemented each other.

054

Minimal outdoor lighting enhances architectural features, and can be used to personalize a home.

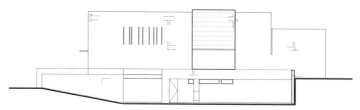

Right side elevation

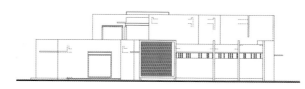

Left side elevation

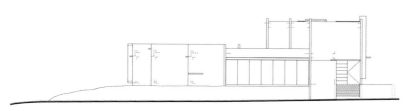

Main elevation

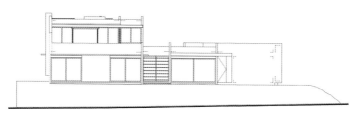

Back elevation

The most-used rooms in this house are on the ground floor. The upper floor is reserved for a studio with an adjacent sitting area, and a guestroom. These spaces have views of the surrounding gardens.

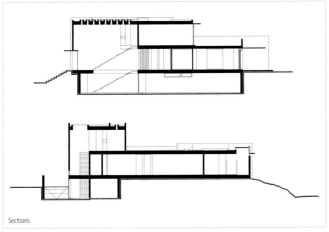

Sections

055

Door handles, screens,
fences, shutters, and railings
are everyday, functional
objects, but can still be given
an artistic design.

056

In minimalist design, wall and ceiling planes have positive forms. This means that space flows around them, instead of them being contained.

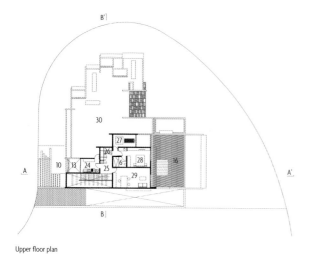

Upper floor plan

1. Garage	16. Terrace
2. Service entry	17. Pool
3. Wine cellar	18. Baby's bedroom
4. Cellar	19. Family room
5. Maid's room	20. Master bedroom
6. Bathroom	21. Bedroom 1
7. Front yard	22. Bedroom 2
8. Garage entry	23. Walk-in-closet
9. Garden	24. Laundry room
10. Entry	25. Vestibule
11. Kitchen	26. Closet
12. Pantry	27. Gymnasium
13. Patio	28. Guest bedroom
14. Dining room	29. Study
15. Living room	30. Roof

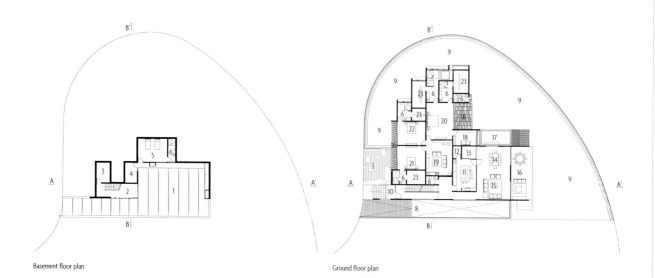

Basement floor plan

Ground floor plan

057

With the addition of seating, a kitchen island offers more than just a preparation surface.

In the hallway near the kids' rooms, privacy is provided by an anodized aluminum screen created by artist Adrián Guerrero.

Rainbow Living

This single-family residence used to be a five-unit apartment building. In developing it, the architects conscientiously used the existing resources, minimizing demolition and maximizing sustainability. Wind and sun provide the house with the energy; light and ventilation promote comfortable living.

Architect: Minarc
Location: Santa Monica, CA, USA
Photography: Courtesy of Minarc

058

Courtyards and patios allow
for natural ventilation, as
do large sliding doors that
open an interior space to the
exterior.

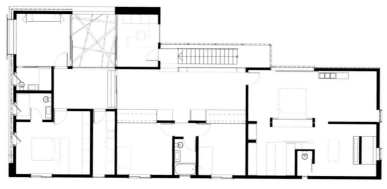

Upper floor plan

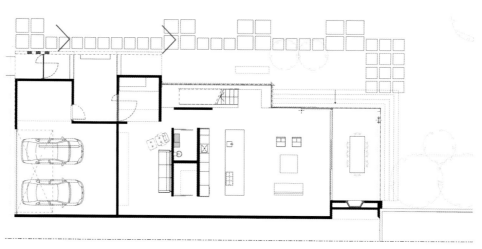

Lower floor plan

059

Reaching innovative
sustainable solutions often
leads to the use of recycled
materials. They can be used
for both decorative and
functional purposes.

Home in Valencia

This project consisted of the extensive remodeling of an apartment for a mother and daughter who work together. The apartment, which accommodates residential and professional functions, includes a large office-library. Having the living quarters at one end and the work space at the opposite end, allows a separation between personal life and work life for the residents.

Architect: **Carmen Baselga_
Taller de proyectos**
Location: **Valencia, Spain**
Photography: **Héctor Rubio**

060

When lining walls with bookcases, keep in mind that that they need to be secured to the walls to prevent them from tipping over.

061

Glass-paneled doors will let light filter through. For example, they can light up a hallway and pour into what would otherwise be dimly lit bathrooms. Use frosted glass to maintain privacy.

062

Translucent resin can be formed into any shape. Examples of interior decorating materials that could benefit from resin are colored plastic, sea shells, small flowers, and pebbles.

Home 08

Architect: i29 | interior
architects

Location: Amsterdam,
the Netherlands

Photography: i29 | interior
architects

The extensive remodel of this small apartment resulted in its resources being
concentrated in two wall units. Entrance hall, toilet room, and closet are contained
in one pinewood-clad volume. A second pinewood-clad wall incorporates a bench,
a fireplace, and storage. The simplicity of the design and materials used give the
apartment a satisfying amount of living space despite its limited floor area.

063

In homes with strict dimensions, bespoke cabinetry enables space saving and an efficient use of difficult corners.

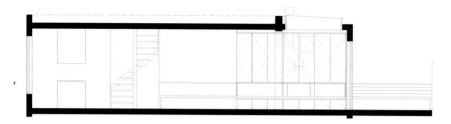

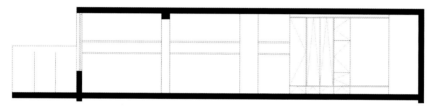

Sections

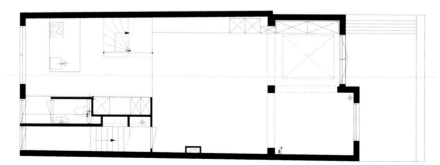

Floor plan

064

In a kitchen, freestanding appliances help break up surfaces. Integrated ones offer a more finished look, but are more difficult to replace.

Tropical White

By luck, Spanish designer Nacho Polo stumbled onto his new house. Built in 1925, it was in serious disrepair due to several hurricanes and years without maintenance. But the house and the gardens that surround it had enough charm left to convince the designer that this was the house he was looking for. Nacho was inspired by the vernacular tropical houses of Key West, Florida, to transform this gloomy old structure into a new light-filled home.

Architect: Nacho Polo
Location: Miami Beach, FL, USA
Photography: Nacho Polo Studio

065

Regardless of style and taste, white brightens up a room and creates the illusion of a larger space.

066

Warm whites are comfortable, while cool whites energize. If you find an all-white room too sterile but don't want contrast, add neutral color accents. You can also play with reflective and transparent materials.

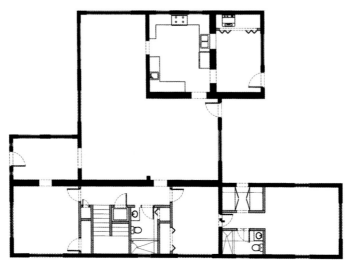

Upper floor plan

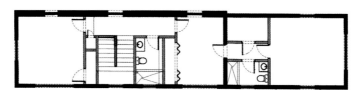

Lower floor plan

067

Pattern and repeated elements
can create a rhythm. Using
them is often sufficient to
make an interesting room
without using a lot of color.

068

Balance is achieved not only
through form, but also through
color, texture, pattern, and
light. The combination of these
elements is how visual interest
is built.

Black on White - Studio House

This house consists of two buildings. One is black with a saddle roof, and the other is a white box. The first cantilevers and is rotated in a way that complements the second. Located on a hillside, the composition intrudes minimally into the natural landscape. The totality of the house is progressively revealed as one descends the gravel slope.

Architect: fabi architekten bda
Location: Regensburg, Germany
Photography: Herbert Stolz

Fully glazed walls in the direction of the wooded valley open the house on both floors. The upper floor, containing the kitchen and living area, has sliding doors that open onto a roof terrace.

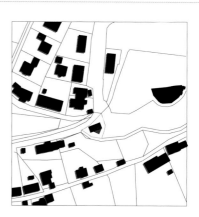

Location map

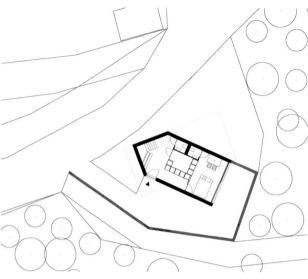

Upper floor plan

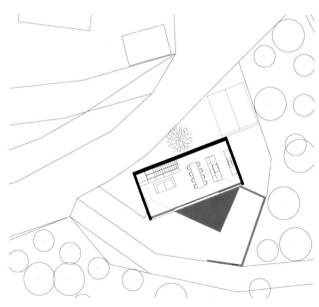

Lower floor plan

069

Matching flooring and furniture materials creates a unifying effect, very suitable for a minimalist interior.

070

An open, floating stair is stylish and sleek. However, the absence of guardrail and the seemingly levitating steps are not suitable for everyone.

071

En suite bathrooms maximize the space of communal areas. Toilets need to be enclosed in a way that satisfies their specific plumbing and ventilation requirements.

308 Mulberry

Architect: Robert M. Gurney
Architect

Location: Lewes, DE, USA

Photography: Maxwell MacKenzie
Architectural Photographer

The starting point for this project was a two-story house built in the early nineteenth century. The spatial needs for the redesign necessitated remodeling the existing balloon-frame house and building four additional structures. The result more than doubled the area of the original house. Its historic base, however, remains prominent.

The additions were conceived of as one-story pavilions arranged around a new swimming pool and a large deodor cedar, which is located at the rear of the property.

072

Large expanses of glass set in
black steel frames are a good
contrasting feature against
a historic, shingle-clad, and
highly detailed construction.

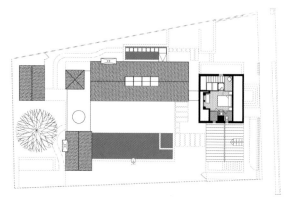

Third floor plan

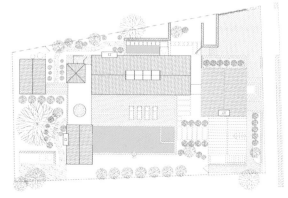

Roof plan

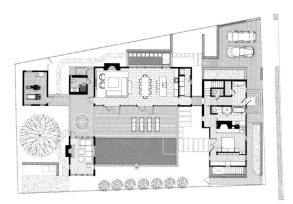

First floor plan

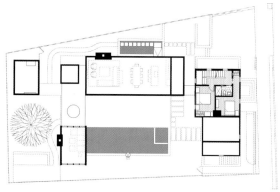

Second floor plan

073

High ceilings, including cathedral ceilings, can cause voices to echo. Wood paneling can dampen sounds in a room with high ceilings and hard surfaces such as glass and stone.

In juxtaposition with the primarily white interiors of the existing house, the new living pavilion features mahogany walls and ceilings and basalt flooring. A white marble fireplace complements it all.

Existing front elevation

Existing rear elevation

New front elevation

New rear elevation

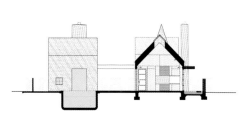

Section

Section

074

Open riser staircases give a stylish and minimalist look to a home. A tempered glass guardrail satisfies safety requirements while maintaining an airy feel.

075

Consider using glass partitions instead of walls, especially in small spaces, to ease the flow of sunlight into a room.

076

An existing structure can meld with new generously proportioned, light-filled spaces, proving that the old can comfortably co-exist with a contemporary style.

Niz House

Faced with the challenge of creating a house on a sloping trapezoidal lot, the architects designed a house with a very narrow front and a wide back façade. One of the sidewalls is angled to align with the staircase, and the effect breaks the orthogonal layout of the house. Because of the pronounced slope of the plot, only minor excavation was needed to bury the garage and utility rooms.

Architect: Agraz Arquitectos
Location: Zapopan, Mexico
Photography: Mito Covarrubias

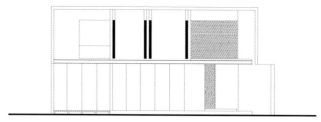

Back elevation

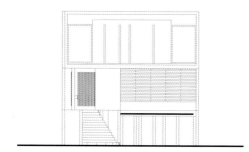

Main elevation

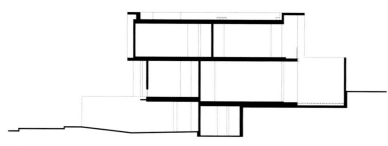

Section

The juxtaposition of the orthogonal grid and the stair built against the angled wall generates void spaces that connect floors and enrich the spatial relationships of the rooms.

077

Make a staircase that stands out by creating a guardrail that also serves as a decorative screen. Lighting will highlight its sculptural quality.

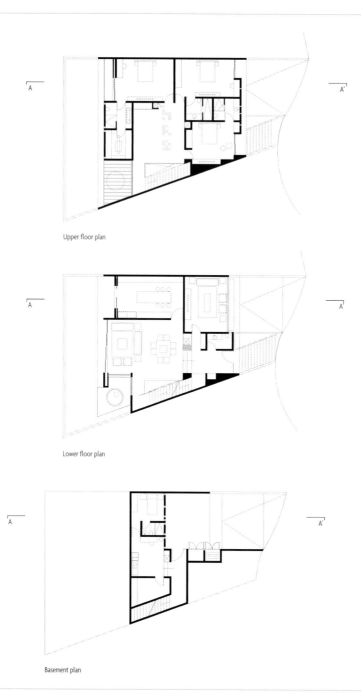

Upper floor plan

Lower floor plan

Basement plan

078

The unusual geometry of the staircase contrasts with that of the rest of the house. Landings, niches, and walls fill in the transitional spaces between the two geometries.

These bathrooms are light-filled spaces.
During the daytime, the creamy white
walls and the white marble countertops
reflect natural light. At night, recessed
lighting and wall sconces keep the rooms
well lit.

Iron House

This project is a remodel of an apartment valuable for its location, configuration, views, and size. The transformation resulted in seamlessly flowing spaces offering a variety of interesting perspectives and a powerful fusion between architecture and interior design. Special care was taken when choosing the materials, to create color and texture contrasts.

Architect: **Filippo Bombace**
Location: **Rome, Italy**
Photography: **Anna Galante**

079

Translucent vertical surfaces are reminiscent of Japanese *shoji* screens. They reveal different spaces, layer by layer, creating an illusion of depth.

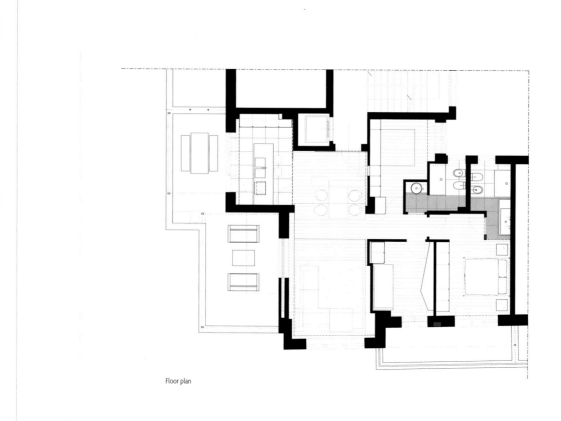

Floor plan

This apartment has balconies on two sides. They constitute an external ring of a radial organization of spaces, the center of which is the rooms that need the most privacy.

080

Sliding screens as we know them are descendants of Japanese rice paper dividers. They allow connections throughout a house and bring a minimalist appeal to rooms.

081

A sink is an important feature of a bathroom. It may have a striking shape, but it should be in harmony with the rest of the room's fixtures.

Hampden Lane House

Architect: Robert M. Gurney
Architect

Location: Bethesda, MD, USA

Photography: Maxwell
MacKenzie Architectural
Photographer

Architect Robert M. Gurney received a commission to build a house for a young entrepreneur who disliked the Craftsman-style house on the plot of land he'd purchased. This led to the demolition of the existing structure on the site. It was replaced by a more environmentally conscious house that provides comfortable, efficient living spaces and embraces a minimalist design.

The house's design was a deliberate departure from the typical architecture of other local homes. It's important to keep in mind what fits a homeowner's unique taste, not just what will make a home blend in.

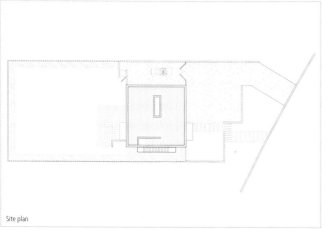

Site plan

North elevation

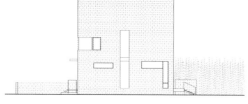

East elevation

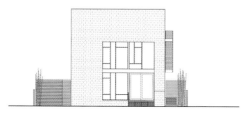

South elevation

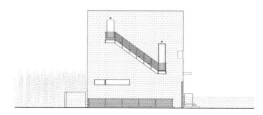

West elevation

Second floor plan

Roof plan

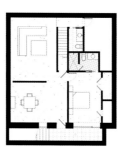

Basement floor plan

First floor plan

Designed as a cube with no unused or underutilized spaces, this house occupies a third less area than the original structure, and was placed to allow the greenery surrounding the house to shine.

082

A minimalist approach to house-planning can maximize the use of available space. Avoid excessive use of partitions and use built-in cabinets instead of armoires and dressers to free up space.

DJ House

Architect: Ivan de Sousa,
Inês Antunes/[i]da arquitectos
Location: Carcavelos, Portugal
Photography: João Morgado

DJ House is located on a small plot in a predominantly residential area. Its architects overcame the challenges of tight dimensions and strict building regulations, to create a space that allows light-filled rooms and visual continuity through voids that seem to be carved out of the house. The simple design of the main façade contrasts with the complexity of the volumes that form the house.

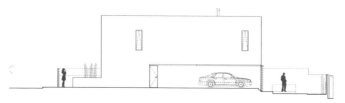

North elevation

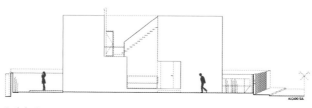

South elevation

East elevation

West elevation

083

Exterior lighting can highlight the architecture of a house or particular features, such as an entry or landscape, while still providing sufficient general lighting.

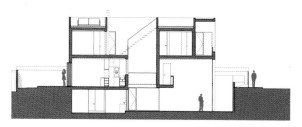
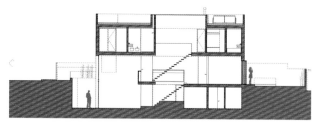
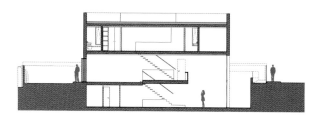
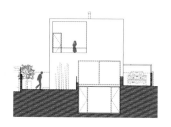

Sections

A central courtyard divides the house into two blocks and helps organize circulation in the interior.

084

Floating stairs have strong sculptural qualities and are reminiscent of the suspended objects made by the American minimalist artist Donald Judd.

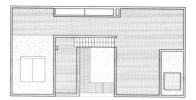

Roof plan

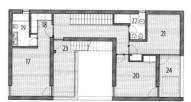

Upper floor plan

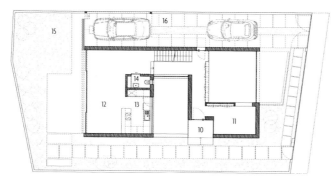

Lower floor plan

Basement floor plan

1. Living room	13. Kitchen
2. Pantry	14. Bathroom
3. Mechanical room	15. Garden
4. Storage	16. Carport
5. Laundry room	17. Master bedroom
6. Storage	18. Walk-in-closet
7. Cellar	19. Bathroom
8. Courtyard	20. Bedroom
9. Courtyard	21. Bedroom
10. Entry	22. Bathroom
11. Office	23. Terrace
12. Dining room	24. Terrace

The living room is a 16-feet-high space. Its placement below street level allows privacy, as well as abundant natural light, which filters in through the courtyard.

085

Glossy finishes highlight architectural features. A combination of glossy and matte surfaces provides depth.

...OM IT ALL) HERE THERE & EVERYWHERE

Hidden Loft

Architect: **KARLA MENTEN |**
architecture
Location: Hasselt, Belgium
Photography: Karla Menten,
Philippe van Gelooven

"Away from it all—here, there, and everywhere" is a quote by American conceptual artist Lawrence Weiner that inspired architect Karla Menten in the design of her home. Menten lives in an almost sterile all-white space, where everything is hidden when not in use. To make it was an arduous design task, as the space is for both living and working.

Menten looked at the suprematist compositions of Kazimir Malevich to inspire the geometry of her home. In her words, her house is "a proposal for a twenty-first century machine for living."

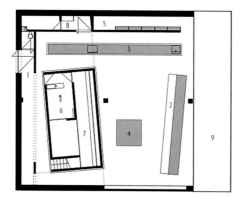

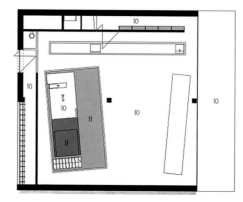

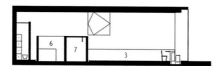

Floor plans and section

1. Entry
2. Table
3. Kitchen
4. Seat
5. Library
6. Bathroom
7. Walk-in-closet
8. Storage
9. Terrace
10. Void
11. Platform

"Away from it all—here, there, and everywhere"
Lawrence Weiner

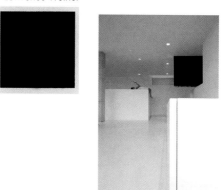

Inspired by the suprematist compositions of Kazimir Malevich

086

Menten's view on "an elementally ethereal aesthetic," a look that involves the retention of open space and a minimum of color, might inspire you if you are disinclined to unnecessary detailing and decoration.

House of Resonance

Architect: FORM / Kouichi
Kimura Architects
Location: Aichi, Japan
Photography: Takumi Ota

The geometry of this two-story house is enhanced by a limited color palette: off-white and jet black. This scheme is carried from the exterior to the interior, where it is used to clearly distinguish different surfaces.

087

Using various shades and tints of the same color adds visual depth. Shades are achieved by mixing a color with black and tints are obtained by mixing with white.

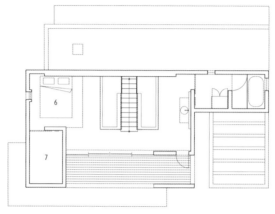

Upper floor plan

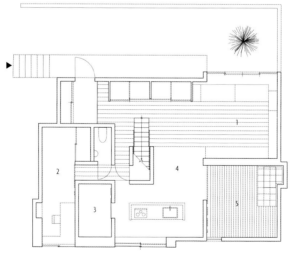

Lower floor plan

1. Living room
2. Kid's room
3. Storage
4. Dining room
5. Terrace
6. Bedroom
7. Closet

Hues that contrast create vibrant spaces. Use this budget-friendly painting trick to dramatically change the look of your home.

A pergola has so much to offer! Whether used as a shading device or a support for climbing plants, it makes an outdoor living room.

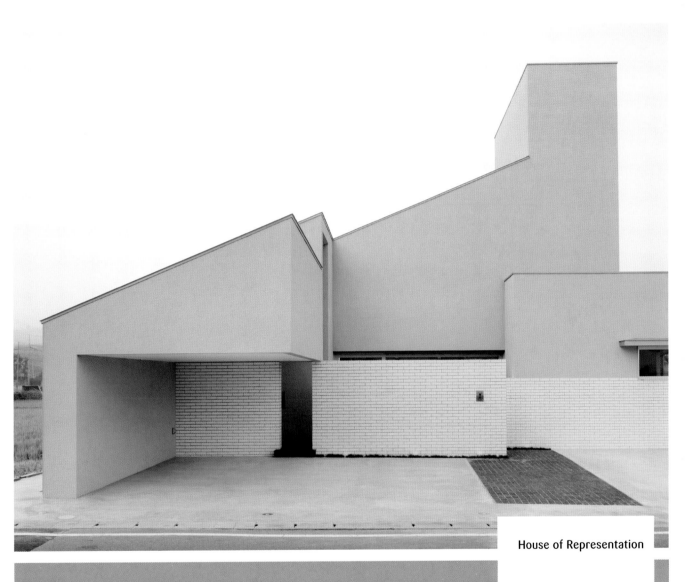

House of Representation

Located in the countryside, this house is notable for its strong geometric features. The design program called for a building that combines privacy and a large living area. With this in mind, the house was given a centripetal layout and a spacious, double-height living room.

Architect: FORM / Kouichi Kimura Architects
Location: Kyoto, Japan
Photography: Takumi Ota

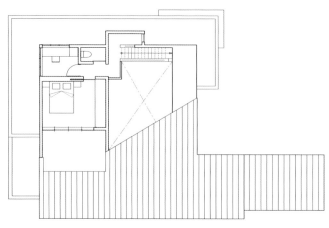

Upper floor plan

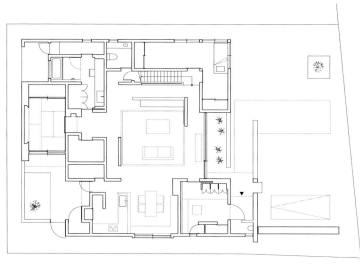

Lower floor plan

090

For a unified, minimal look stick to a single color range and a limited selection of materials. Choose neutral shades to create a serene atmosphere.

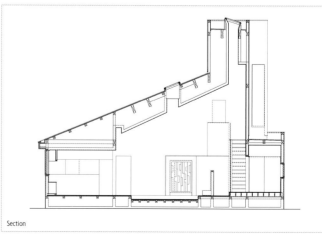

Section

091

Keep in mind that flush
transitions between different
flooring materials are difficult
to obtain. To achieve flush
surfaces you might have to
provide a variable subfloor.

The geometry of a space can be emphasized by a subtle combination of white-painted surfaces, concrete, stone, and wood, and light to cast a glow on these elements.

House of Reticence

This new construction satisfied the client's request for a house that provides both privacy and a sense of openness. The house has a layered orthogonal layout defined by interlocked spaces, and a zigzagged façade that adapts to the triangular shape of the site. The elongated vistas give a feeling of spaciousness. The thoughtfully positioned openings allow privacy.

Architect: FORM / Kouichi Kimura Architects
Location: Shiga, Japan
Photography: Takumi Ota

092

Low furniture accentuates the horizontality of a long rectangular space. To further emphasize this type of design, avoid wall-hung cabinets that would obstruct sightlines.

The "rooms" are not enclosed, but rather screened-off by a well-thought-out orthogonal arrangement of walls.

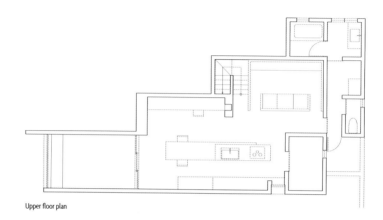

Upper floor plan

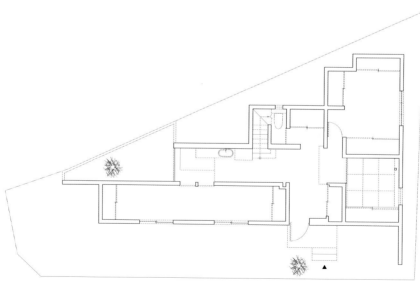

Lower floor plan

093

In addition to providing a sense of spaciousness, an open-plan layout allows light from the perimeter to reach the inner reaches of a space.

094

Keep your bathroom counter clutter-free to let the material shine in its own light. A limited amount of carefully chosen items can be used to complement the décor and create a casual elegance.

Small House

Architect: FORM / Kouichi
Kimura Architects
Location: Aichi, Japan
Photography: Kei Nakajima

Commissioned by a middle-aged couple, this house is a quiet retreat away from the tumult of its densely populated neighborhood. Despite the limited dimensions of the site, the architect successfully created a spacious interior. The living room, the central space, has the tallest ceiling in the house and is surrounded by the kitchen, dining room, and bedroom.

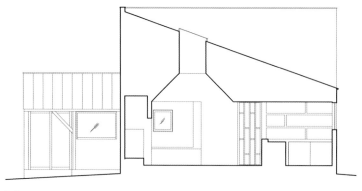

Section

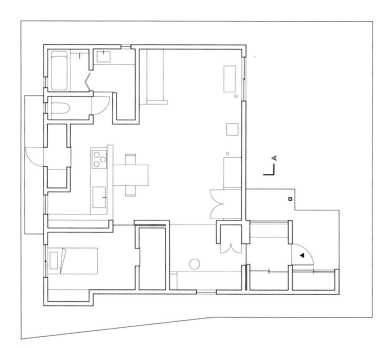

Floor plan

095

One of the advantages of built-in furniture is that it is often built along walls, freeing up space to aid order and tidiness.

096

Different functions of spaces in an open-plan home can be defined by a change in flooring materials or in floor and ceiling heights. Freestanding furniture can also break up a space.

097

Polished concrete can be used for a variety of services, such as for flooring or a wall finish, or for built-in furniture such as countertops and shelves.

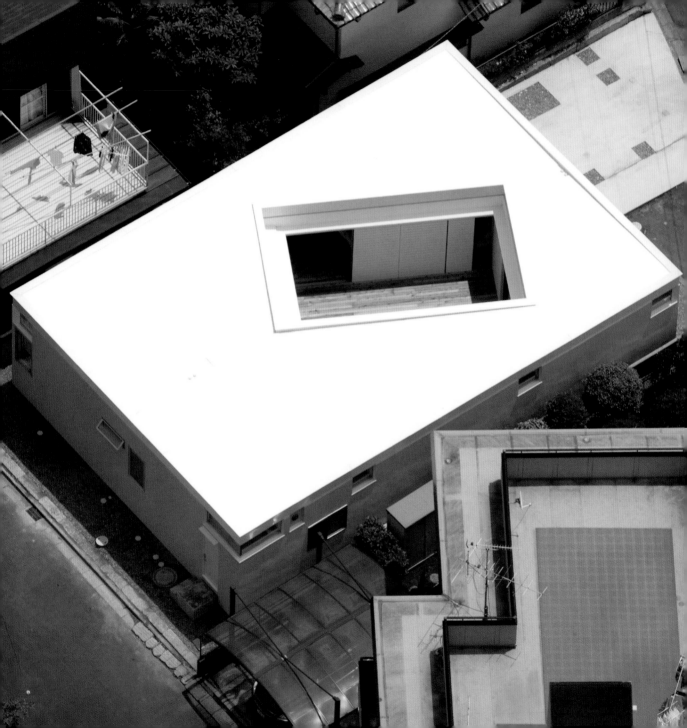

F-White House

The courtyard in this single-story house gains prominence from its skewed position in relation to the house footprint. The oblique position of the courtyard is not the outcome of a capricious design decision, but rather a response to a functional need. Had the courtyard been inserted orthogonally, the house would have been divided into two blocks. Instead, with the courtyard turned at an angle, a sense of unity is maintained.

Architect: Takuro Yamamoto
Architects

Location: Kashiwa City,
Chiba, Japan

Photography: Ken'ichi Suzuki
Photo Office

098

This design reflects the minimalist principle that voids and negative spaces are just as important as masses and positive spaces.

The space around the courtyard feels like a room with different functions at every turn of the corner. This feeling is heightened by the lack of hallways and vestibules.

099

The use of sliding doors
and low walls that show
the continuity of the ceiling
creates a minimalist, loft-like
environment.

Stripe House

Architect: GAAGA

Location: Leiden,
the Netherlands

Photography: Marcel
van der Burg

Stripe House takes its name from the horizontal grooves across the entire envelope
of the building. Located at the end of a row of houses, it is a three-story home that
offers views of the surrounding landscape from a variety of directions.

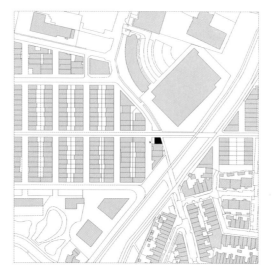

Location map

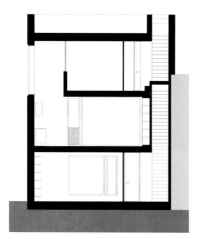
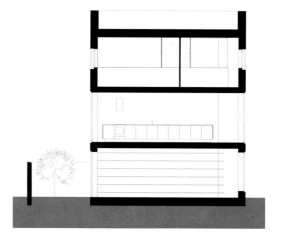

Sections

Despite the small size of this site, which is located in an urban area, its ground floor has both a studio and a garden. The latter is a transitory space between the street and the indoors.

A large living area and a kitchen occupy
the second floor. There, a tall space along
the kitchen wall connects this floor with
the one above containing two bedrooms
and a bathroom.

100

Double-height spaces are worth the sacrifice of square footage, as they spatially enrich a room. The addition of a clerestory or high window will distribute light evenly throughout a room.

Second floor plan

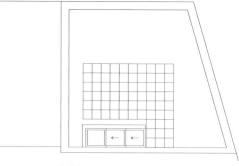

Roof plan

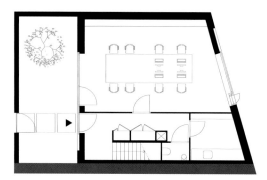

Ground floor plan

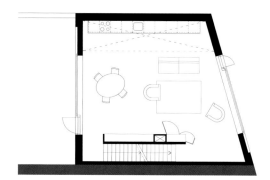

First floor plan

101

Vertical houses maximize views and sunlight. Make the most of higher floors by creating light-filled rooms, stacking utility rooms and staircases to do so.

World Flex Home

Using advanced technology, worldFLEXhome creates modular housing that can be adapted to meet individual needs and be used to build villas, townhouses, or clusters of houses. Its structures include environmentally friendly elements, such as green roofs, solar energy, and eco-conscious heating and cooling systems.

Architect: AY ArcgencY
Location: Wuxi, China
Photography: Jens Markus Lindhe, Mads Møller

102

An island can be beautiful and highly functional, with a clean working area and plenty of storage—maybe even open shelves.

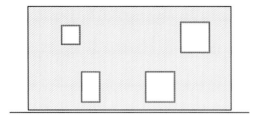

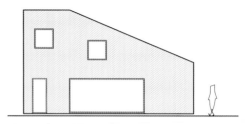

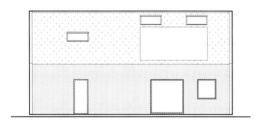

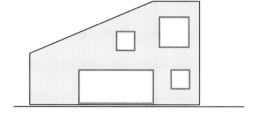

Elevations

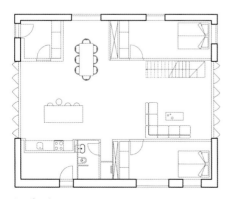

Lower floor plan

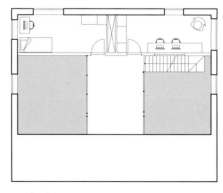

Upper floor plan

103

A window with a vision line into kids' bedrooms or playrooms will help parents keep an eye on them. To make the window childproof, the glass needs to be tempered.

Ballymahon

Architect: ODOS architects
Location: Longford, Ireland
Photography: ODOS architects

A new single-story construction completes the courtyard once formed by three eighteenth-century farm buildings and replaces a stone wall that was in extreme disrepair. In contrast with the massiveness of the existing stone, brick, and slate buildings, the addition features large expanses of glass allowing visual connection between the courtyard and the surrounding woodlands.

The oiled cedar cladding connects
the new construction with its wooded
surroundings, and warms the courtyard.

104

An open layout accentuates the linearity of a room. To break up a long space alternate surfaces such as walls and floor-to-ceiling windows.

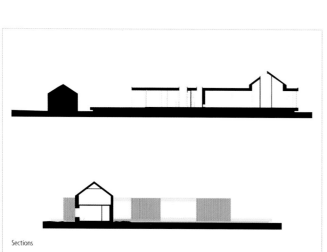

Sections

The use of epoxy-polished concrete
flooring links the new building to the old
ones made from stone, brick, and slate.

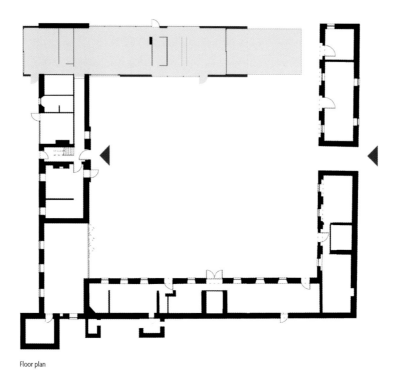

Floor plan

105

The new wing, which has been skewered through one of the existing farm buildings, is raised off the ground to give it a floating quality.

Cove lighting is built into valences, ledges, and recesses. It enhances ambient lighting without breaking the uniformity of a ceiling.

Architect: METAFORM
architecture

Location: Luxembourg,
Luxembourg

Photography: Steve Troes
Fotodesign

This seven-unit residencial building is constructed in a compact space in a suburb marked by how spread out its buildings are. It was created in a discreet manner, and its simple exterior finish matches the building's monolithic appearance.

The varying volumes merged with the
continuous grid of the façade, blurring
the differentiation of the stacked floors.

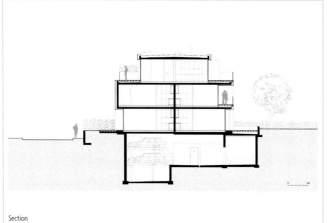

Section

Second floor plan

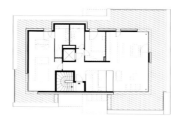

Third floor plan

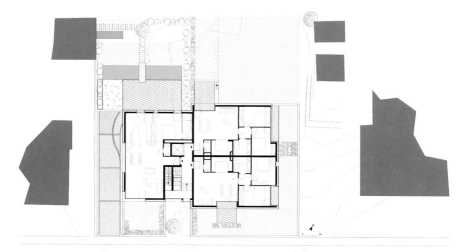

First floor plan

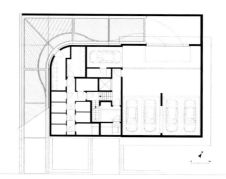

Basement floor plan

106

Position windows to maximize interesting views. If a space allows, use floor-to-ceiling ones to allow in as much natural light as possible.

107

Use glass instead of solid walls in en suite bathrooms. They let light in and make a room look bigger.

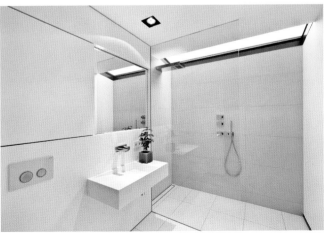

108

Plumbing instruments are indispensable bathroom elements. For a minimalist design, select contemporary ones that have clean and smooth surfaces.

White Apartment

The design of this spacious apartment was a response to the client's request for a place to relax and enjoy family life. With a primarily white and gray palette, and marble floors and lacquered furniture, it bestows a sense of luminosity. RGB LED lighting enhances this.

Architect: Chalupko Design
Location: Warsaw, Poland
Photography: Monika Zielska

109

American minimalist artist Dan Flavin embraced fluorescent tubes in his work. The striking lighting effects they create can be inspiring when you are considering the atmosphere you'd like a room to have.

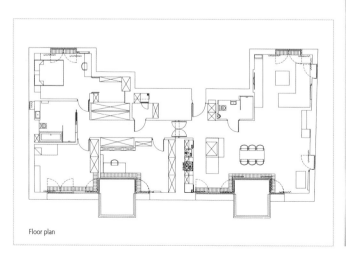

Floor plan

110

A high-gloss lacquer finish is typical of art deco furniture, but can also provide a contemporary room with a sleek and sophisticated look.

111

Colored lighting can enliven a room or a narrow hallway where there is little opportunity for furnishing.

112

The wall behind a headboard can be used to make a design statement, and light can be part of it. Indirect lighting produces a soft glow that can help you create a calming atmosphere.

Superba

Architect: Minarc
Location: Venice Beach, CA, USA
Photography: Minarc

This innovative construction responds to the growing demand for customizable and affordable housing. Making use of prefabricated elements and efficient, modular manufacturing, its design is well-integrated. The limited number of preassembled parts that were necessary for its construction is what makes this house affordable.

113

The flexibility of building parts in modular construction allows for a custom-made home fitted to a specific location and homeowner's needs.

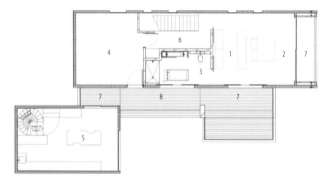

Upper floor plan

1. Open walk-in
2. Bedroom
3. Bathroom
4. Music studio
5. Jewelry studio
6. Hall
7. Covered veranda
8. Terrace

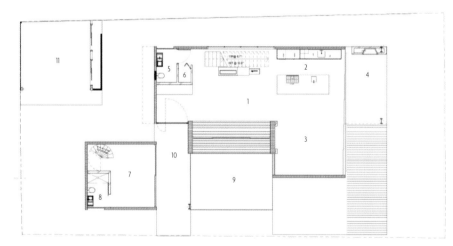

Lower floor plan

1. Living room
2. Kitchen
3. Family room
4. Veranda
5. Powder room
6. Laundry
7. Guest room
8. Bathroom
9. Pond
10. Entry
11. Carport

114

The affordability of a modular building lies in limiting the number of assembled elements, eliminating custom on-site fabrication.

115

High-quality materials, a wide variety of design options, and a fast construction timeline have made modular housing popular.

116

Consider designing with materials that can be easily reused for future projects. This can apply to small-scale projects, such as furniture design, or larger-scale undertakings, like buildings.

Villa Allegra

Architect: Oppenheim
Architecture + Design

Location: Miami, FL, USA

Photography: Laziz Hamani,
Eric Laignel

Multiple rooms, both interior and exterior, were added to what was originally a nondescript one-story home, and take advantage of Miami's tropical weather. The design was based on an abstract interpretation of historical elements common in neighboring homes, where exterior spaces are just as important as interior ones.

Elevations

The entry to this house is through a 20 x 30 x 30-feet volume where a reflective pool, echoed by an opening in the roof, highlights the space with a scattered, reflected light.

Roof plan

117

Make the most of the richness and warmth of wood. Let it take center stage against a backdrop of white walls.

118

The remodeling of this house
was intended to emphasize its
comfort and fun.

119

Do not clutter a large room with an excess of furniture. A few well-chosen pieces make a greater impression when surrounded with space to breathe.

House in Futakoshinchi

This is an example of how Japanese architects often deal with small spaces. The house is located at the end of a long, narrow driveway, and occupies a 15.7 x 24.2 x 26.9 foot volume split into six levels. Two stairwells topped by skylights and small wooden step-boxes connect the different levels.

Architect: **Tato Architects**
Location: **Kanagawa, Japan**
Photography: **Mitsutaka Kitamura**

120

Split-levels can divide a floor with varying functions; for example, raising the floor of a living room will separate it from a dining room.

Second floor plan

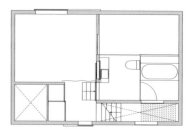

Third floor plan

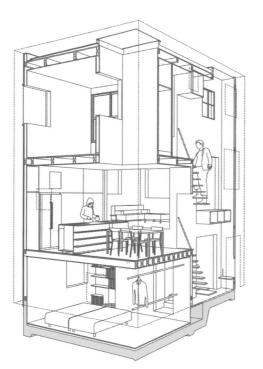

Axonometric view

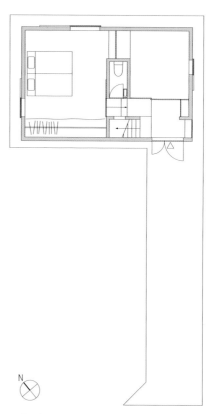

N

First floor plan

121

Step boxes, often associated with Japanese aesthetics, connect spaces of different heights. They eliminate the need for constructions that would disrupt the simple geometry of a room.

122

Raising a bathroom floor can help accommodate plumbing underneath, create an interesting floor level change, and even allow for a sunken bathtub.

123

Consider using curtains instead of doors to hide the interior of a closet. They add texture and soften a room.

This house consists of two "boxes" separated by a central glazed stairwell. These two boxes contain living areas and bedrooms that alternate with courtyards and lightwells. Openings on the exterior walls are relatively small and sparse, just enough to establish connections with the surroundings, giving the house an introverted character.

Takanawa House

Architect: Hiroyuki Ito Architects

Location: Minatoku, Tokyo, Japan

Photography: Daici Ano

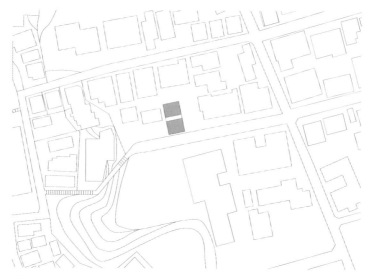

Location map

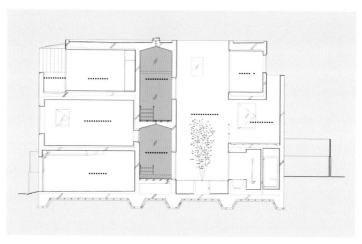

Section

The stairwell is board-formed concrete, matching the finish of the building's exterior. The surfaces in the rooms are painted white.

124

A well-lit room has light coming in from at least two directions— for example, from windows on different walls or from a skylight and a window.

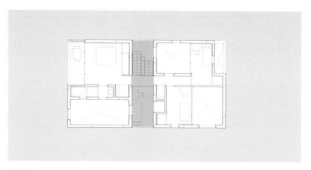

Third floor plan

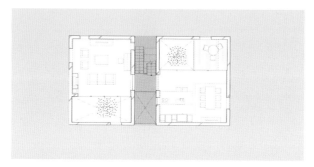

Second floor plan

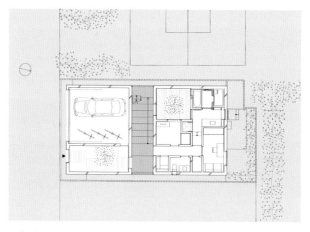

First floor plan

125

In courtyards of small or awkward dimensions, a sharp and sophisticated design can be created with marble chips and a small selection of plants.

Beaumont House

The Beaumont House is a duplex residential building situated in a mix-use neighborhood where residential units coexist with small to mid-size industrial buildings. Its concrete skin, exposed on the exterior and in the interior, is its most distinguishing feature. Each unit contains a large, double-height living room composed of concrete and wood surfaces, which act as foils to each other.

Architect: **Henri Cleinge Architecte**
Location: **Montreal, QC, Canada**
Photography: **Marc Cramer**

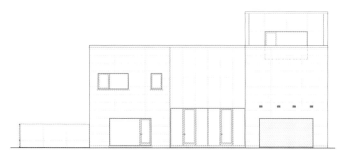
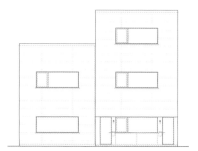

Elevations

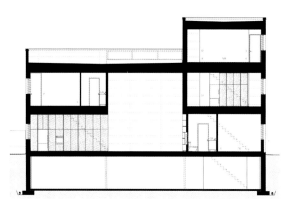

Section

The layout of the duplexes allows
each unit to take advantage of
southern sunlight.

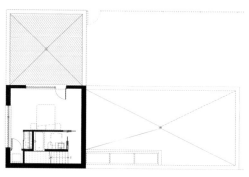

Third floor plan

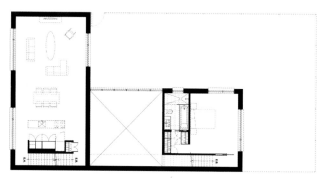

Second floor plan

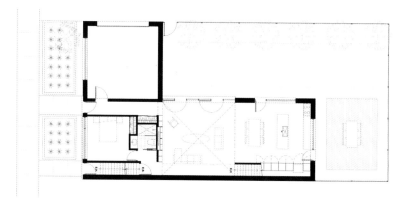

First floor plan

126

Concrete deflects sound; wood
and fabric absorb it better
because they are much softer.
Consider using them to minimize
reverberation.

127

Using only concrete in an interior space can make it feel cold. In combination with wood, which adds a sense of comfort and warmth, it can make a space seem honest and simple.

128

Textures play an important role
in interior design. They can be
rough or smooth, hard or soft,
matte or glossy. Vary them and
create contrast with opposites.

House in Ookayama

Architect: **Torafu Architects**
Location: **Tokyo, Japan**
Photography: **Daici Ano**

The first part of a two-phase project for the refurbishment of a forty-year-old, mixed-use, reinforced concrete building, involves the design of the building's exterior and the apartments on its second and third floors. Towering above the surrounding houses, the third floor accommodates well-lit living spaces, while the second floor offers more private spaces.

129

Like steel, the versatility of
concrete allows it to be used for
a variety of purposes, not just
structurally. One way to use it
is as a finish material.

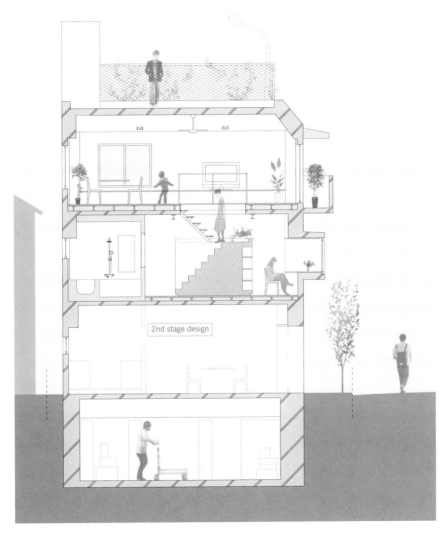

2nd stage design

Sectional diagram

130

Furnishings can be seamlessly integrated with architecture; they can also be removed or altered according to a homeowner's needs. This allows the possibility of a continually adapting environment.

131

To make a unique kitchen, mix
and match different woods on
drawer and door fronts, but
use a unifying element such
as handles and knobs.

This freestanding cube incorporating a stair and a closet was designed to avoid the compartmentalization of an open plan. Its central location helps to organize circulation.

By concentrating the stair and a closet in a freestanding cube, the rest of the loft-like space is left unobstructed.

Gable House

Architect: FORM / Kouichi
Kimura Architects
Location: Shiga, Japan
Photography: Takumi Ota

Two major concerns conditioned the design of this house: noise and climate. Since the site is located along a high-traffic road, it was insulated to provide a peaceful environment. The simple, boxy shape and the pitched roof protect it from the effects of frequent snowfalls.

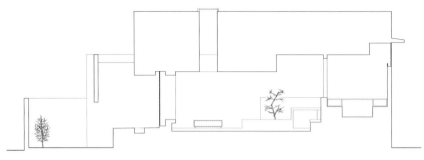

Section

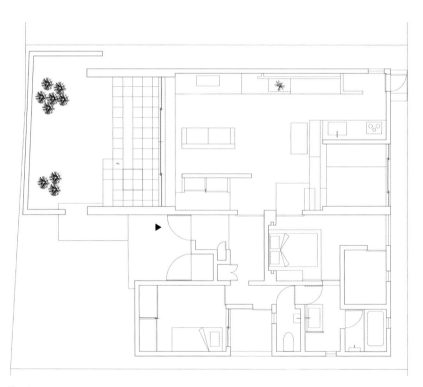

Floor plan

The yard of this single-story house is screened-off from the street to mitigate car noise. Above the yard, a hanging wall extends views from the interior into the yard while providing privacy from passerby.

132

Xeriscape landscaping, a method of landscape design for arid areas, easily complements a minimalist design.

The house has few windows, but various
skylights provide illumination.

A secluded area is perfect for meditation or yoga.

Rather than blending in with the neighboring small, traditionally designed houses, this house is monolithic and monumental. It was built from concrete and dark-colored brick, and its few openings give little indication of what its interior is like. The limited selection of materials used to create it in combination with the rays of light piercing through it, creates a monastic atmosphere; thus the name, the House of Silence.

House of Silence

Architect: FORM / Kouichi
Kimura Architects
Location: Shiga, Japan
Photography: Takumi Ota

This two-story house is a complex composition of interlocking volumes that create positive and negative spaces. These spaces capture light, contributing to the spaciousness of its interiors.

The interior is characterized by
diaphanous spaces, courtyards, and
different floor levels and ceiling heights.
Interior and exterior framing achieves
a surprising effect.

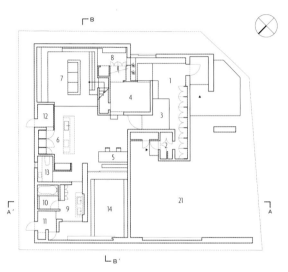

Lower floor plan

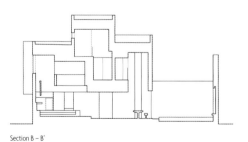

Upper floor plan

1. Formal entrance
2. Family entrance
3. Hall
4. Guest room
5. Dining room
6. Kitchen
7. Living room
8. Study
9. Powder room
10. Bathroom
11. Pantry
12. Storage
13. Toilet
14. Terrace
15. Void
16. Master bedroom
17. Closet
18. Hobby room
19. Kid's room
20. Balcony
21. Garage

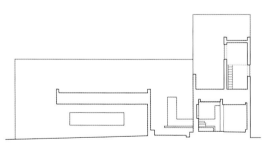

Section A – A'

Section B – B'

134

Dark floors ground a room, drawing attention downward. High ceilings make it look more spacious and give it an airier feel.

135

Set panels off walls and emphasize soffits and dropped ceilings. These tricks highlight the contrasting effect produced by a new construction inserted into an existing shell.

136

Black steel has a black oxide coating. It is a good material for producing furniture because of its thin profile and its attractive dark patina, which offers a sophisticated look suitable for modern interiors.

137

With frameless windows, the glass area is maximized to make the most of views and natural light. The minimalist window system integrates into the façade with its almost invisible fittings.

Costa Esmeralda House

Architect: María Victoria
Besonías, Luciano Kruk/
BAKarquitectos
Location: Costa Esmeralda,
Argentina
Photography: Gustavo Sosa Pinilla

This site, in an area of coastal dunes, has a slight depression at its center and a row of tall acacias along the street. These features provide the homeowners with privacy. The design took advantage of the height difference between the street and the center of the lot to create two stacked structures forming an L-shape, with the living area at the top and the bedrooms at the bottom.

Northeast elevation

Northwest elevation

Southwest elevation

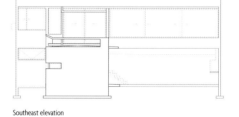

Southeast elevation

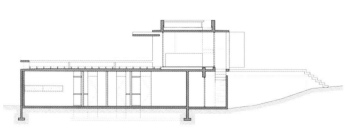

Sections

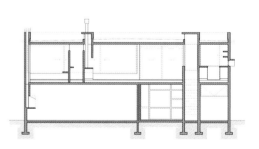

138

A detailed sun path analysis that outlines the shaded areas of a home is critical for optimizing the benefits of a brise-soleil.

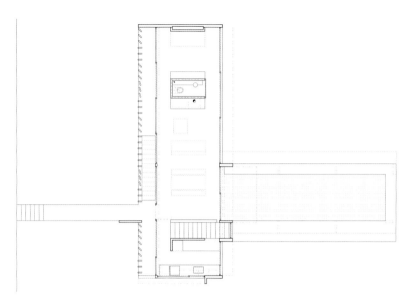

Upper floor plan

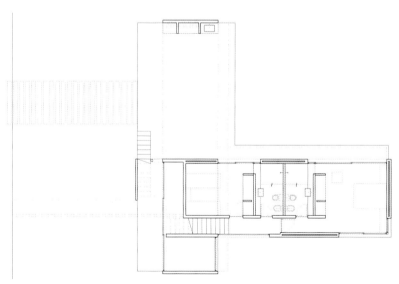

Lower floor plan

139

A brise-soleil forms a double-skin in front of a fully glazed enclosure. The structure avoids excessive heat from the sun, while letting in abundant natural light.

140

A backsplash window in a kitchen brings in plenty of light over the countertop and still leaves room for shelves above.

141

Hand-packing concrete produces veining. If this technique is used in a room where water penetration is a concern, such as a bathroom, the concrete surface should be finished with a coat of polyaspartic.

The features that make this house unique are: its response to a steep slope, the privacy it offers—especially street side, and its success in making a small area habitable by minimizing circulation spaces.

Franz House

Architect: María Victoria Besonías, Luciano Kruk/ BAKarquitectos

Location: Mar Azul, Argentina

Photography: Gustavo Sosa Pinilla

The house is very compact, developed on two floors, and built into the hillside. Like the other local houses designed by its architects, it blends beautifully with the wooded landscape.

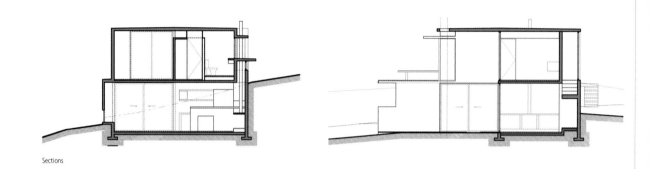

Sections

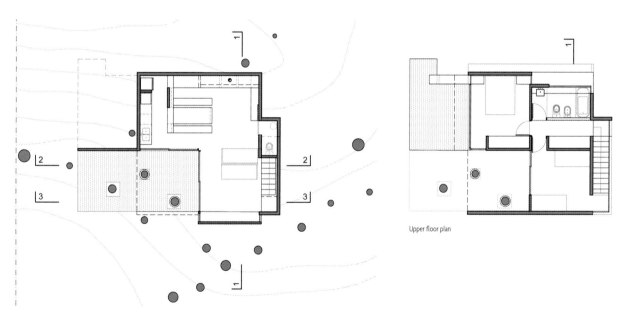

Lower floor plan

Upper floor plan

142

In architecture as in art, form, light, and the qualities of materials are the essence of minimalism. In the words of architect Ludwig Mies van der Rohe: "Less is more."

143

Exterior and interior spaces received equal attention. Outside the living area, a double-height porch was build around two pine trees, reinforcing a connection with nature.

144

Use glass to maximize natural lighting, to establish visual connections, and to create a sense of unity among different spaces.

AV House

Architect: María Victoria Besonías, Luciano Kruk/ BAKarquitectos

Location: Mar Azul, Argentina

Photography: Gustavo Sosa Pinilla

The gradual but constant grade of the terrain dictated the orientation and design of this house. The result is a cluster of stepped concrete structures, each serving a different function. The plan, which follows an east-west axis, generates two clearly differentiated façades. The entry is at a central location and separates the living areas from the bedrooms.

145

The shape and orientation of a house impacts its comfort and energy efficiency. Houses with simple designs are usually more energy efficient than those with complex shapes.

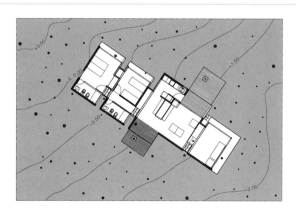

Floor plan

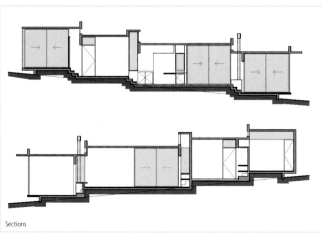

Sections

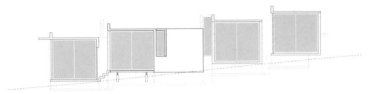

North elevation

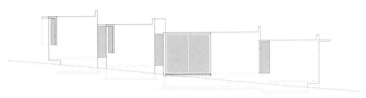

South elevation

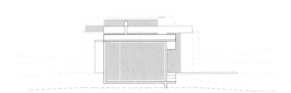

West elevation

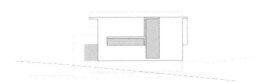

East elevation

146

A shell uniquely composed of
two materials, concrete and
glass, integrates this house with
the surrounding environment
and resolves structural and
functional issues.

The few interior walls are made of hollow
brick and finished in concrete screed.
Except for the beds, couches, and
chairs, all of the house's furnishings
are concrete.

147

Concrete is a versatile material that provides a wide range of finishes. Both smooth and rough concrete can be stained, dyed, troweled, stamped, and polished to a high gloss.

Carling Residence

Architect: TACT Architecture

Location: Northern Muskoka,
Georgian Bay, ON, Canada

Photography: Terence Tourangeau

Particular care was taken in placing this house to take optimum advantage of the landscape's natural features, which provide shade and privacy, while still allowing spectacular views. The house's minimalist design, with its glass façades, makes it blend nicely with its surroundings.

148

Large trellis overhangs might be just what you need above your windows in order to screen off bright sunlight.

149

To make a ceiling seem higher, use a dark wainscot. If the wainscot is recessed relative to the face of the wall, the wall will cast a shadow on the wainscot and the heightening effect will be even stronger.

150

A restrained material selection of stone, wood, concrete, and white-painted walls contribute to the elemental feel of a house.

Minimalist interiors complement rugged surroundings, enhancing the landscape and making it an integral part of the design.

DIRECTORY

AGI Architects
Safat, Kuwait; Madrid, Spain
www.agi-architects.com

Agraz Arquitectos
Guadalajara, Mexico
www.agrazarquitectos.com

AY ArcgencY
Copenhagen, Denmark
arcgency.com

Carmen Baselga_Taller de proyectos
Valencia, Spain
www.estudiocbaselga.com

Chalupko Design
Warsaw, Poland
www.chalupkodesign.pl

DUE Architecture + Design
Ibiza, Balearic Islands, Spain
due-studio.blogspot.com.es

EMPTY SPACE Architecture
Lisbon and Oporto, Portugal
www.emptyspace.pt

fabi architekten bda
Regensburg, Germany
www.fabi-architekten.de

Filippo Bombace
Rome, Italy
www.filippobombace.com

FORM / Kouichi Kimura Architects
Kusatsu, Shiga, Japan
www.form-kimura.com

**Fran Silvestre, Mª José Sáez/
Fran Silvestre Arquitectos**
Valencia, Spain
www.fransilvestrenavarro.com

GAAGA
Leiden, the Netherlands
www.gaaga.nl

Henri Cleinge Architecte
Montreal, QC, Canada
www.cleinge.com

Hiroyuki Ito Architects
Shinjuku, Tokyo, Japan
www.ofda.jp

i29 l interior architects
Duivendrecht, the Netherlands
www.i29.nl

**Ivan de Sousa, Inês Antunes/
[i]da arquitectos**
Lisbon, Portugal
www.i-da.eu

**Jakub Majewski, Łukasz Pastuszka/
Moomoo Architects**
Warsaw, Poland
moomoo.pl

Jorge Hernández de la Garza
Mexico City, Mexico
www.hernandezdelagarza.com

KARLA MENTEN | architecture
Hasselt, Belgium
www.karlamenten.be

Marià Castelló
Formentera, Spain
www.m-ar.net/ct

María Victoria Besonías, Luciano Kruk/
BAKarquitectos
Buenos Aires, Argentina
www.bakarquitectos.com.ar

METAFORM architecture
Luxembourg, Luxembourg
www.metaform.lu

Minarc
Santa Monica, CA, USA
www.minarc.com

Nacho Polo
Miami Beach, FL, USA
www.nachopolo.com

ODOS architects
Dublin, Ireland
www.odosarchitects.com

Oppenheim Architecture + Design
Miami, FL, USA; Basel, Switzerland
www.oppenoffice.com

Pitsou Kedem Architecture
Tel Aviv, Israel
www.pitsou.com

Robert M. Gurney Architect
Washington, DC, USA
www.robertgurneyarchitect.com

Swatt | Miers Architects
Emeryville, CA, USA
www.swattmiers.com

TACT Architecture
Toronto, ON, Canada
tactdesign.ca

Takuro Yamamoto Architects
Shinjuku, Tokyo, Japan
takuroyama.jp

Tato Architects
Kobe, Hyogo, Japan
tat-o.com

Torafu Architects
Shinagawa, Tokyo, Japan
torafu.com

Vitor Vilhena arquitectura
Lagos, Portugal
www.vitorvilhena.com